George Jamieson

The Silver Question

Injury to British trade and manufactures

George Jamieson

The Silver Question
Injury to British trade and manufactures

ISBN/EAN: 9783744735216

Printed in Europe, USA, Canada, Australia, Japan

Cover: Foto ©Suzi / pixelio.de

More available books at **www.hansebooks.com**

THE SILVER QUESTION.

INJURY TO BRITISH TRADE AND MANUFACTURES.

THE PAPER

BY

GEORGE JAMIESON, Esq.

(H.B.M.'s Consul-General at Shanghai, China),

WHICH WON THE BIMETALLIC PRIZE OFFERED BY SIR HENRY
M. MEYSEY-THOMPSON IN 1894;

TOGETHER WITH

TWO OTHER PAPERS ON THE SAME SUBJECT

BY

THOMAS HOLYOAKE BOX
(YOKOHAMA);

AND

DAVID OCTAVIUS CROAL
(LONDON).

ALSO

A PREFACE AND SEQUEL

BY

SIR HENRY M. MEYSEY-THOMPSON, BART., M P.

1895.

LONDON : EFFINGHAM WILSON, ROYAL EXCHANGE, E.C.

PRICE SIXPENCE.

PREFACE

By Sir Henry Meysey-Thompson.

In introducing to the public the following excellent papers on the subject of the injury done to the trade and manufactures of England by the divergence in value between gold and silver, I will say only a very few words in explanation of my reasons for offering a prize.

Fifteen years ago I had come to the conclusion that if the value of gold, as measured by silver and commodities, were to continue to rise, the inevitable consequence must be the banishment of all our great manufacturing industries from England, to find a home in the silver-using countries of the East and elsewhere.

This theory I and others proclaimed from the housetops, but we found that we might as well have been crying in the wilderness; no one would listen to us. Yet the theory is very simple, and seemed to us quite conclusive.

What is the question? It is one simply and solely of locality. The manufactures of the world will certainly be carried on *somewhere:* where is that *somewhere* to be?

Now, we have all to make up our minds:

(1) Do we *wish* that the home and principal seat of the great manufacturing industries of the world—the cotton, woollen, worsted, linen, jute, iron and steel, machinery, leather, clothing, pottery, glass, and many others, including all our existing agricultural industries—should continue to be in the United Kingdom, as hitherto, and that they should be carried on by English, Scotch, Irish, and Welsh workmen; or do we *wish* to see them banished to the soil of India, China, Japan, and Mexico, and carried on by Indian, Mexican, Chinese, and Japanese workmen?

(2) Is it certain that our present monometallic policy *must* drive these industries away from the soil of the Unite

Kingdom, and cause them to be carried on, instead, on the soil of India, China, Japan, and Mexico.

Let us compare England and China in the year 1869, and again in 1894, to take a round quarter-century of time. Let us suppose that an independent capitalist, resident, say, in America, and caring nothing either for England or China, were hesitating in which country to set up a manufactory. Let us suppose that he made inquiry as to the cost of labour in the two countries, and that he was told the amount of labour required to make a given quantity of cloth would cost him one sovereign in England, or 4 ounces of silver in China, he would say : " The value of silver is 5s. per oz. : 4 ounces of silver cost £1 : my sovereign would purchase the same amount of labour either in England or China. I prefer England."

Now let us look at 1894. Gold wages have certainly not fallen in England ; we have conclusive evidence that silver wages have not risen in China; therefore, if the same man inquired now, he would still be told that the labour required to make a given amount of cloth would cost him one sovereign in England, or 4 ounces of silver in China. He would say : " Silver has fallen from 5s. to less than 2s. 6d. per oz. ; therefore, for *half-a-sovereign* I can buy 4 ounces of silver, and, as far as the cost of labour is concerned, I can now get as much cloth made in China for half-a-sovereign as I can get made in England for a sovereign. I prefer China."

The public would not stop to listen ; but "dogged does it." We hammered away, making a convert here and there, until now even Sir William Harcourt admits that the professors of Political Economy are on our side. During the last two years, I have had information sent me from many parts of the world, that the manufacturing and agricultural industries in silver-using countries are advancing by leaps and bounds; while in England and other gold-using countries they are mostly stagnant and declining.

Now, I said to myself, we have no longer to rely on theory; we have hard practical facts to point to. *Someone* should put these facts in a way in which our great industrial population can understand them. Let them once grasp the fact that employment is slipping from their hands into those of Chinese and Japanese, and the thing is done.

The hour has come: can we find the Man? It was in order to find the Man that I offered my prize. I hope that the readers of these Essays will agree that in Mr. Jamieson, H.B.M.'s Consul-General for China, excellently supported as he is by Mr. Croal and Mr. Box, the man is found.

CONDITIONS OF THE PRIZE.

SIR HENRY MEYSEY-THOMPSON offers a Bimetallic prize of a silver cup or silver plate value £25, and £25 in sovereigns, for the paper which points out most clearly and plainly :—

(1) The great loss and injury which is being inflicted on the producers of this country by the extraordinary rise in the value of gold as compared with that of silver during the last twenty years, consequent on changes in the laws regulating the use of gold and silver as money in various countries.

(2) The immense temptation and inducement which this rise in the value of gold holds out to capitalists in silver-using countries, to develop their coal mines, and to erect machinery for the purpose of supplying themselves and other silver-using countries with the manufactured articles which this country has for long been in the habit of supplying them with.

(a) When the result of this rise in the value of gold has been a rise in the silver price of our manufactures.

(b) When the result has been a fall in the gold price of them.

(3) That in the competitive manufacturing industries of the world this divergence of value between gold and silver must inevitably lead to the substitution of the cheap labour of silver-using countries for the more highly paid labour of gold-using ones, a substitution which is already rapidly taking place, and which, unless some international agreement is come to at once, must lead to the ruin of many of our industries, and the throwing out of employment of tens of thousands of our workmen.

All the papers must be in English, and either printed or type-written, and be sent in before the 30th September, 1894, to Sir Henry Meysey-Thompson, M.P., Kirby Hall, York.

No paper must exceed in length twelve pages of the "Nineteenth Century Review."

The right is reserved to Sir Henry and to the Bimetallic League to publish or reprint all or any part of the article which wins the prize in any form they please, without any further payment to the author of it.

BIMETALLIC PRIZE COMPETITION.

Paper submitted by

GEO. JAMIESON, H.B.M. Consul-General,
Shanghai, China.

WINNER OF THE PRIZE.

VIEWING the world as a whole, the observed facts during the past twenty years may be stated as follows :

(1) Prices (wholesale) of nearly all commodities have fallen in gold-using countries. This fall coincided roughly, step by step, with the fall in the gold value of silver up to the end of 1892. Since that date silver has fallen more rapidly than commodities, but the latter appear to be still falling.*

(2) Wages, rents, and taxes in gold-using countries have not varied, or have varied only within narrow limits, due to temporary and local causes. Agricultural rents should, perhaps, be excepted ; but these are subject only to periodical revision.

(3) Retail prices (into which wages, rent, and taxes enter largely) have not fallen to the same extent as wholesale prices, in many cases they have not fallen at all.

(4) Prices (wholesale) of all commodities in silver-using countries have remained approximately steady during the

---

*Index No.   1892, Silver 65·4, Commodities 68.
Sauerbeck's Tables, Ap. 1894   ..   46·8,   ,,   63

period, and this whether the articles were produced in the country itself, or imported. In the case of articles imported from gold-using countries, however, there has been, since the middle of 1893, a rise in silver prices, corresponding to the divergence between silver and commodities noted in No. 1.

(5) Wages, rent, and taxes have not varied in silver-using countries, or have varied only within narrow limits, and from causes unconnected with the relation of gold to silver.

(6) Retail prices in those countries have not varied, except in the case of articles purchased retail in gold-using countries, which have risen in proportion to the rise in gold.

In so far as these propositions refer to facts observable in England, it is unnecessary to offer any remark with regard to prices and wages in silver-using countries, especially the Asiatic countries, which are by far of the greatest importance to us, I would refer to the following publications :

"Prices and Wages in India." Statistical Department, Calcutta, 1893.

"Prices of Commodities in China." Consular Reports. Miscellaneous Series, No. 305, 1893.

The various statistical publications of the Chinese and Japanese Governments. It is impossible in this short paper to do more than indicate the data.

The first question is, in what way and to what extent have producers in England suffered loss by the demonetization of silver ?

The loss to producers is the lowered value of their produce, while wages, rents and all outgoings remain the same as before.

What, then, are the causes which have contributed to lower the prices of commodities in England and other gold-using countries, specially of agricultural produce?

Any alteration of prices must be due to causes affecting the demand, or to causes affecting the supply, or to changes in the currency itself.

It will readily be admitted that there is no falling off in demand. The world generally, is growing in wealth and population, and so far as demand alone is concerned prices should be rising. The cause or causes must therefore be sought in the other two elements.

The causes are, I would submit, the following, and I enumerate them in what I consider the order of importance as affecting agricultural produce, beginning with the one which has the least effect.

(1) The first is cheap ocean freights, and a lessening of cost of production, through improvements in machinery, new chemical discoveries, and other scientific advances.

(2) The appreciation of gold, consequent upon the demonetization of silver.

(3) An enlarged area of supply consequent on the relative cheapness of silver to gold. As silver prices in Asiatic countries have not risen, the produce of those countries can be laid down in England at almost Asiatic prices.

I shall briefly remark on each of these in order.

(1°) Lowered cost of transport and production. This cause is often put forward as being the principal element in the case, and it is necessary to notice it, as it has doubtless had some effect. But it may be pointed out, that this cause, or set of causes, rather, had been in operation long before 1873, and did not prevent a great rise of prices between 1850 and 1873. Had these been the only agents working for a fall, all other things being equal, though in some commodities the fall might have been considerable, it is very

4

improbable that prices all over would have been reduced more than a few points, possibly 3 to 5 per cent.

(2°) The appreciation of gold.

It will readily be admitted that if gold were the only currency in the world, a sudden augmentation or diminution of the mass, by, say, one half, would raise or lower prices in nearly the same proportion. Now when gold and silver circulated side by side, at a fixed ratio maintained by the open Mints of the Latin Union, the metallic medium may be deemed to have been, for all practical purposes, either all gold or all silver. For example, suppose there are x oz. of gold in circulation, as currency in the world, and y oz. of silver, and that one oz. of gold exchanges for sixteen ounces of silver; then the metallic medium, in terms of gold, would be $\left(x + \frac{y}{16}\right)$ ounces, and in silver, would be $(16x+y)$ ounces. The two terms would be perfectly interchangeable, and the world might be said in effect to be monometallic. Prices in gold would adjust themselves in relation to the mass $\left(x + \frac{y}{16}\right)$, and prices in silver in relation to the mass $(16x \; y)$, and how much was x, and how much was y, would be perfectly immaterial. Relatively to one another the volume of either might vary indefinitely, without having any effect upon prices, which would vary only in relation to the mass of the two.

Such in effect was the state of the world up to 1873. The value of the whole of x was then, as we know, approximately equal to the whole of y; but that was quite accidental, and had not always been so.

By the breaking of the Bimetallic link, the silver-using and the gold-using portions of the world parted company. In the gold-using portion, prices began to adjust themselves in relation to the mass x, and in the silver-using portion in relation to the mass y, or, to speak more correctly, in relation to that mass of y which, for the time being, entered into their currency.

Now, had the two halves of the world been approximately equal in wealth, population, and extent of commerce, the adjustment might have been effected without any great disturbance of prices. One would have parted with its gold, and the other with its silver, as a fair exchange, and no harm would have been done to anybody.

As a matter of fact, however, the two halves were very unequal, the gold-using half being immensely superior; and, moreover, this half was owner of a great part of the floating silver, and of the silver-producing mines. Anxious as gold countries might be to get rid of their surplus silver, they would not part with it for nothing; and ready and anxious as silver-using countries might be to get silver, they could only get it for value of some sort, either by way of loans, or in settlement of the annual balance of trade. This is a process that takes time. Silver-using countries for the most part are making additions to their stock of silver, year by year; but they are absorbing it only slowly. Consequently prices in those countries conform themselves, not to the whole mass of y in the world, but only to that part of it which has found its way into their circulation.

I may remark here in passing that this seems to explain quite satisfactorily how it is that prices and wages have risen so little in those countries, contrary to what was generally expected. In India, where the additions to the currency have been considerable, there has been some rise in the price of food and wages, particularly in those classes of skilled labour which the new industries have called into existence. So in Japan the same thing may be observed in a smaller degree. In China, on the contrary, there has been no import of silver to speak of, and no change whatever in prices and wages. Nor is there likely to be any material change in this respect, whatever the relative value of gold and silver may be ; though, of course, the lower silver goes, the easier in a way will it be for China and the other silver countries named to get it.

In gold-using countries, on the other hand, which have voluntarily restricted their circulation to gold, inasmuch as the mass x is manifestly insufficient to carry the commerce and industries formerly borne by x plus a considerable portion of y, prices, of course, have fallen. The quantity x has to be spread over a greater area, and as the annual additions are only sufficient to repair waste, and to meet the increased demand due to the natural growth of trade, the value necessarily appreciates.

What the exact percentage due to this cause may be I do not venture to attempt to estimate. Whatever it may be, it ought to affect all commodities alike, and also, though more slowly, wages.

(3°) The other cause which I have named, has been and continues to be the principal factor in cheapening the prices of produce, especially produce of the cereal class.

A very few words will suffice to make this clear. In the years preceding 1873, when the rupee was at 2s. nearly, the price of Indian wheat in Bombay was approximately 10s. per cwt., and the *Gazette* price of English wheat in London was about 54s. per quarter, equal 12s. 4d. per cwt. Allowing for quality and costs of transport, these prices may be deemed equivalents. When the rupee exchange fell to 1s. 6d., Indian wheat, the silver price of which in Bombay has with temporary fluctuations, remained constant,* would cost in Bombay about 7s. per cwt. and could be laid down in London for

---

* Official quotation. Wheat No. 1, soft, per candy 1873 R.34 8 0
  „   „   „   „   1893 R.32 11 1
  Prices and Wages in India.

something like 8s. 6d. All the other sources of supply remained open as before, the supply for the time being was greater than the demand, and consequently the price fell to the level of the lowest market. Again the exchange value of the rupee falls to, say, 1s. 1d. Indian wheat can now be laid down in London at nearly half the sterling price of 1873 (costs of transport having also in the meantime been greatly reduced), and consequently the price of wheat all over falls to a corresponding point.

This is a fair illustration of what has been going all over the world. We draw our supplies from all countries wherever they can be procured most cheaply. By each successive drop in the gold value of silver, a greater and greater amount of produce has been admitted from India and other silver countries, and always at a cheaper rate. Had the rupee retained its old value, of 2s., it is perfectly certain that no wheat could be imported from India at present rates. There is no reason to suppose that the rupee price in Bombay would have been materially different from what it has been. Had the gold value of the rupee not fallen, the area of grain supply would never have widened as it has done, demand and supply would have been more evenly balanced, and the variations in price would have been confined within small limits.

The same reasoning that applies to grain applies to every other article that can be supplied freely from silver-standard countries. The silver prices in those countries have, as the experience of twenty years has shown us, remained approximately steady, and necessarily the gold price has fallen. In no article, however, has the correspondence between the price of silver and the price of the article been so complete as in grain. In 1873, when the price of silver was 60d., wheat stood at 54s. To day silver is 28½d. and wheat 24s., being

c

.a drop in the one case of 52·5 per cent., and in the other of 55·6 per cent.

It is simply the old law of supply and demand. Increase the area of supply, and you have, for the time being, the supply outrunning the demand. With an excessive supply the cost of production in the cheapest area must determine the price of the whole. So long as Indian wheat can be laid down at 23s. a quarter it is impossible for English farmers to get a higher price, quality for quality. India, by itself of course, could not provide enough wheat to supply the whole English demand, but that is not the point. All the other sources, whence England drew her supplies before the fall in silver, still continue to send wheat forward, and it is the cheap rate at which the excess supply from India and other silver countries is offered, that governs the market The lower silver goes the cheaper and cheaper does this excess supply become. And there is no help for it, until either silver begins to rise again, or until some portions of the earth are thrown out of wheat cultivation, and the demand again overtakes the supply.

But it may be said, granting that the cheapening of produce is hard on the agriculturist, it must be a very good thing for the country at large, especially for the manufacturing portion, who get the same wages, and therefore can live so much better. This seeming prosperity, however, can be but short lived, for—

II. The rise in the value of gold hoids out an immense temptation to the capitalists of silver countries to develop their coal mines, and to erect machinery for the purpose of supplying themselves and other silver countries with the manufactured articles which this country has long been in the habit of supplying them with.

The inducement to this lies in the fact that wages in all silver-using countries, formerly cheap, have now, by the

fall in silver, become fifty per cent. cheaper, relatively to gold
wages, or, to put it in a different form, that wages in gold-.
using countries have, through the appreciation of gold, become
100 per cent. dearer than they were relatively to silver wages.

Prices of commodities regulate themselves automatically,
and from day to day. Given an equilibrium of prices at
any moment between a silver-using and a gold-using
country, any subsequent fall in silver must have one or
other of two results: either the gold price must fall, or
the silver price must rise. The exchangeable value of any
article is, within a certain limit, representing costs of
transport, necessarily the same all the world over. A bale
of cotton, for example, has the same exchangeable value
in Liverpool, Bombay, or New Orleans, allowing for a certain
fixed margin, representing costs of transport, merchants' profit and duty, if any. In bulky articles this margin is of
course considerable, but that does not affect the principle.
Whenever the a.ticle, for any reason, becomes cheaper in one
place than in another, there is a profit in exporting it. A
flow sets in from the cheaper to the dearer, until the ordinary
equilibrium is restored.

With wages, however, it is different. The price of a day's
labour in Bombay bears no relation to the price in Liverpool,
even assuming the quality to be equal. If, indeed, we could
import a cargo of coolies as easily as we import a bale or
cargo of cotton, the adjustment would be rapid. But the
standard of wages in any country is regulated on very
different principles. The law of supply and demand, which
governs wages, is not international, like the law for commodities, but national or even provincial. And in England
where the rights of labour are so well guarded by trade-
unionism, and a sympathetic legislature, even the law of
supply and demand has not free scope. An employer of
labour must pay the recognised wages or close his mill.

c2

Adjustments in the direction of a fall, can only be brought about by concerted action, and usually after a strike or lock-out. or other painful and expensive process.

Let us see now, how these principles work out in our trade with silver using countries, say China, to take a familiar example.

The result of a fall in silver must be, as I have said, that either the silver price in China must rise, or the gold price in England must fall, or else it must be partly the one and partly the other. An English merchant who ships cotton manufactures to China, can only do so on terms that pay in the long run. If the buying price in Manchester keeps firm, he must get such a higher silver price in China, as will counteract the fall in exchange. If silver falls ten per cent. he must demand a ten per cent. higher silver rate, other things being equal ; if the Manchester market falls ten per cent., he will be able to sell at the old silver rate, or if the Manchester market falls 5 per cent., he will be content with a 5 per cent. rise.

The observed course of prices, during the twenty years up to the end of 1892, has been that gold prices have fallen, and silver prices have remained steady. Since the beginning of 1893, however, there has been a change. The Manchester price has been steadier, and consequently the silver price has risen. The following table compiled from the published market reports in Shanghai, shows the variations in silver prices of Manchester goods for the last fourteen years. The prices of 1882 are taken as 100.

1882	 100	1889		 100
1883	 98	1890		 95
1884	 99	1891		 97
1885	 99	1892		 99
1886	 99	1893	June......	115
1887	 103	1893	Dec.......	139
1888	 108	1894	June......	138

The rise, as will be seen, was as much as 33 per cent. Possibly this will not be maintained, but undoubtedly a very considerable rise, which looks like being permanent, has been established.

Let us consider, firstly, the effects when the gold price falls, and by consequence the silver price is steady.

Suppose two cotton mills working, the one in England, and the other in Japan or China, and competing with one another for the sale of their productions, and contrast the position of the two in 1873 and in 1893. Let us assume that in 1873 they were competing on even terms, that is, that each realised to the owners the same profit. In 1894 each employs the same amount of labour as it did in 1873, which the English pays for in gold at the old rates, and the Japanese in silver also at the old rates. The Japanese mill-owner still pays for his men, as he used to, 18 to 20 cents a day, and for his women 8 to 10 cents a day. In 1873 that meant 9d. to 10d. per day for men, and 4d. to 5d. for women. Now, it means just one-half, that is, 4d. to 5d. and 2d. to 2½d. Multiply this over 2,000 mill hands, and see what the saving will be on labour alone. But this is not all. The same advantage accrues on the coal bill. Japanese coals cost them, say, $4 to $5 a ton, which meant 16s. to 20s. They still can be got at $4 to $5 a ton, but that now only means 8s. to 10s. The same thing applies to rent, wages, taxes, and all fixed charges whatsoever. They are all payable in silver, and have nowise varied with the rise in gold. Only in the single item of raw material is the old equality maintained. Both are free to buy that wherever they can find it cheapest on the world's market, the only advantage being proximity to the best source of supply and, consequently, economy of transport.

Now, so long as the gold price went on falling, and the silver price consequently kept steady, there was no great manifest advantage resulting to the Japanese manufacturer from a fall in exchange. He continued to get the same prices for his products, and his outlay was the same, year by year, both being in silver. Any improvement he could effect by economy of management or by getting his raw material cheaper, would be so much extra profit, otherwise his position was unaffected. In any case exchange fluctuations would not trouble him.

The English manufacturer on the other hand, has to meet the same fixed expenditure from ever decreasing returns. He is able to buy his raw material cheaper, owing to the general fall in commodities, but his wages bill, his rent, his interest on borrowed capital, his rates and taxes, have all to be met as before. His profits begin to dwindle, it is only by the greatest economy of management that he can keep open at all. The best mills only manage to pay a fair profit, the worst struggle to the verge of bankruptcy, always hoping for a turn of the tide, and finally are forced to close.

Suppose, in the second place, that the silver price rises, and, as a consequence, the gold price remains steady.

The gold manufacturer is, for the time being, in an easier position. His returns do not fall off, and, though his expenses are the same, he is in a position to profit by any economy of manufacture or management.

But the silver manufacturer is, so to speak, on clover. All his working expenses are on the old scale, and he is thus a clear gainer by the extra price he gets for his products. If silver prices have risen, say, 10 per cent., his profits will be increased by just 10 per cent. on his turnover. The natural result of this will be to attract more capital, more mills will be built, and the output will increase. Competition will lower prices, and the gold manufacturer will again be driven into a corner.

Whatever happens, the manufacturer in the silver standard country, has a great advantage, and simply for this reason, that he can obtain his labour at half the cost relatively to gold wages, which he formerly paid. And this advantage must remain to him (unless silver can in the meantime be brought back to something like its old value) until either wages in gold countries have fallen 50 per cent., or till they have risen 100 per cent. in silver-using countries, or till some common meeting ground has been found between the two In other words, the old equilibrium will not be restored until the standard of living and comfort, amongst the working classes in England, has greatly fallen, or till the standard in silver-using countries has greatly risen.

There is only one item that militates against the manufacturer in silver countries, and that is the enhanced cost of his new machinery. It so happens that at present all, or nearly all, manufacturing machinery has to be procured from England or Europe, and the lower silver goes the more of it do Eastern manufacturers require to purchase this portion of their plant. As to this, I would only make two remarks. In the first place the gold price of machinery has itself greatly fallen with the general fall in prices. In the second place, the dearer machinery is the better will it pay silver capitalists to make that too in their own country.

In the foregoing discussion, the form of industry specially in view was the manufacture of textiles, but it will be apparent that the same argument applies to the making of machinery, and, indeed, of almost every article which we have been in the habit of supplying silver countries with. In all industries where rough mechanical labour forms a principal ingredient, there is an obvious advantage. The building and repairing of ships might be quoted as an instance, and it is worthy of note that at the last annual meeting of one of our steamboat companies, the chairman informed his shareholders that a large saving had been effected by having their ships docked in the East instead of in England.

The same stimulus is given to open coal mines, and to develop the natural resources of those countries. If native and foreign coal, twenty years ago, sold at about equivalent rates, the former would be to-day some 50 per cent. cheaper, simply through currency changes. And as a matter of fact, it is now well known that the whole trade of the East is supplied by Japanese and Chinese coal. The former, indeed, is being sent to San Francisco and Bombay, and the time may not be far distant when it will be sent through the Canal and even to England itself.

III. The result of all this must be that in the competitive manufacturing industries of the world the divergence of value between gold and silver will inevitably lead to a gradual transfer of the seat of all the great manufactures from gold-using to silver-using countries, and, if England persists in excluding herself from the benefits of an abundant supply of the international media of exchange, to the ruin of our national industries.

As competitors with one another for the sale of their products on the world's market, the nations that can for any reason produce most cheaply are bound to win in the long run. Hitherto we have been able to do this from a combination of causes. Cheap iron, cheap coal, scientific improvements in machinery, skilled workmen, and economy in the combination of labour, have for a long time enabled us to maintain an industrial supremacy, and yet to pay our workmen higher wages than were paid in any other country. And had this currency trouble never arisen, there is not the least doubt but that we should easily have held our own.

But the momentous economic change implied in the divergence of the old value of gold and silver by as much as 50 per cent., has entirely altered the conditions.

Coal is not any longer relatively cheap in England, nor is iron. Labour is 100 per cent. dearer in relation to silver wages than it was. We have no monopoly of scientific machinery. Oriental nations can buy the best that is produced, and they can engage skilled workmen to teach the natives how to beat us at our own trade.

And though I have insisted on the element of wages as being, as I believe it is, the most important factor in the case, it is not the only advantage that silver-using countries have. Rents, taxes, rates and all fixed obligations whatever, are light and easily discharged, whereas in gold countries they are heavy, and tend to become heavier with every further appreciation of the metal.

The consequence of all this is what might be expected, while old-established industries in England are in many cases barely paying expenses, new and rival industries in the far East are springing up broadcast, and, in spite of inexperience and extravagance of management, are paying handsome returns to their owners.

In the report of the Yokohama Chamber of Commerce, dated May 5, 1894, the following statistics are given.

The first spinning mill in Japan was erected in 1863 with 5,456 spindles.

At end of 1883 there were 16 mills with 43,700 spindles.

,,	1888	,,	24	,,	88,140	,,
,,	1892	,,	39	,,	403,314	,,
,,	1893	,,	46	,,	about 600,000	,,

The same report adds, as till more rapid increase is expected in the near future, large orders, it is known, have been placed for more machinery, some for yarns of the finer qualities.

In the Consular Report on trade at Kobe, for 1892, a return is given of the dividends paid during the preceding 12 months by 21 mills in Osaka, the average dividend was

18 per cent. the highest being 28 per cent. and the lowest
8 per cent. The dividends for 1893 as reported from time
to time, in the Japan newspapers, appear to have been equally
good or better. According to a recent number of the Japan
Gazette, eleven mills whose names are given, paid an average
dividend of 16 per cent. for the first six months of 1894, as
compared with 12 per cent. for the corresponding period
of 1893.

Compare this with the account of the cotton trade in England, as given in the *Economist* of February 17, of this year.
I cannot afford room to quote passages, but, briefly, the balance-
sheets of 93 spinning companies in Oldham show a net total
loss of £72,768 in 1893, against a like net loss of £104,664
in 1892. At the end of 1890 only eight of these companies
had adverse balances, and these amounted to only £8,412;
at the close of 1891, 49 companies had adverse balances,
amounting to £142,767; and at the close of 1893, 63 companies had realised a total loss of £366,800 on their working
account.

Surely there is something seriously alarming in these
figures. Have our manufacturers, with all their accumulated
wealth of experience, become so effete that they allow themselves to be beaten at their own trade by amateur spinners in
Japan? Or is it not that there is some enormous difference
in the economic conditions of the two countries, which
enables the Eastern manufacturer to win without effort, while
the Western is struggling his hardest to get even a place in
the race.

It has not unfrequently been said, that it is some consola-
tion to us, in the midst of all our depression of trade, to find
that other countries, such as Germany and the United States,
are in an equally bad condition. But I would venture to
suggest that this exactly emphasises the present contention,
viz.: that the countries that are suffering by reason of the

all in silver, are the gold standard countries, and those that are reaping the benefit are the silver countries.

If India is pointed to as a silver country, that is in an embarrassed condition, I would reply that the whole of her trouble comes from the fact of her owing a large foreign debt in gold, which is quite accidental. Had her debt been payable in silver, as it might have been, and but for her relation to England probably would have been, she would now be in an excellent position. Taxation, in that case, would have been light; trade and manufactures would have been increasing, as they are, and all circumstances would have been favourable to the rapid accumulation of wealth.

China, which has long lagged behind in the industrial race, is also waking up to the situation. At the present moment three large factories are being erected at the port from which I write, covering many acres of ground, and before another year is out, two or three hundred thousand spindles will be at work. That the ordinary Chinese coolie can be readily converted into an efficient mill hand has been abundantly proved. His patient endurance of labour is well known, as also his frugal habits. The present rate of wages, with which he is well content, may be put, in English money, at from 3d. to 5d. per day. The supply of labour is so enormous, and the extent of the country is so vast, that many years must elapse before there can be any material rise in wages.

But it may be urged, granting that India and other Eastern nations can make their own coarser and commoner yarns and cloths, the competition is after all confined to these grades, and they cannot touch us in the finer qualities. It is no doubt true, that hitherto the competition has been mainly in the class of goods mentioned, but there is no reason whatever why it should be confined to that. If there is any force at all in the argument adduced, it extends to all industrial operations whatever. The only reason why Eastern mills have hitherto devoted themselves to the lower counts of spinnings is that native cotton is most suited for this quality, and that the greatest profit was to be made in this branch of the industry. But there is no reason why American and Egyptian cotton should not be imported when required, as it is imported into England. No doubt a good many years will elapse before these Eastern mills can oust us from the position we now occupy as manufacturers of the medium and finer fabrics. But that things are tending that way, there can be no doubt. Mr. O'Conor, Assistant Secretary to the Government of India, in his Review of the Trade for 1892-3, says :—

" The influences that affected the market for yarns, affected also the market for piece goods, which continue to exhibit a non-progressive character. The trade in unbleached goods is smaller than it has been since 1883, and in neither white nor coloured goods is any advance apparent for many years. It must be inferred that, as suggested in the Review of Trade for 1890-1, imported piece goods are gradually being superseded by local manufactures."

And again, page 36.

" There is no doubt, looking at the course of trade over a series of years, the competition of Indian mills is telling on the import of Manchester goods. The mills are gradually beginning to make the medium class of goods, which form the bulk of the imports, and they are also beginning to bleach and dye their goods."

The process described by Mr. O'Conor, will be hastened by the development of yarn spinning, in the far East. The principal outlet for Bombay yarns has been China and Japan. As these markets are closed to them, as they will be in a few years by the progress of local mills, the Bombay mill owners must devote themselves more and more to the medium and finer kinds of cloth, which in turn will oust the Manchester products.

But the object of this paper is not to show the rate of speed at which these changes may be expected to arrive, but to show the tendency and drift of things, as the inevitable consequence of the monetary disturbance. There are, of course, other elements that count, and which may for a period postpone the catastrophe, or mitigate its effects. Intelligence, organization, abundant supply of capital may enable a manufacturer to hold his own, or even to succeed against economic advantages favouring his competitor. England has all these on her side, and doubtless will make a good fight for it.

But our manufacturers are fighting against odds. They are handicapped in the race, and many changes and adjustments are inevitable. Many forms of industry will have to be abandoned altogether, and though new forms may take their place, much capital will be lost, and much suffering entailed.

But why should our people be handicapped? What national advantage can be shown at all commensurate to the great evils that are evident? It has, unfortunately, become ingrained in the English mind, that gold monometallism is inseparable from our national prosperity. But should we not have prospered all the same up to 1873 had we been Bimetallic as France was? We should have enjoyed all the advantages of a fixed par of exchange none the less, by being ourselves a party to the League. And has the nation prospered so much since 1873 that we are justified in glorying in monometallism? Some individuals have prospered, no doubt. All those who have a realized capital in gold have benefited. But for the bulk of the nation, for the industries which are the life and soul of the country, the change has been almost an unmixed evil.

GEO. JAMIESON.

THE RISE IN THE VALUE OF GOLD.

BY

THOMAS HOLYOAKE BOX,

YOKOHAMA.

THE RISE IN THE VALUE OF GOLD.

BY

THOMAS HOLYOAKE BOX.

———

(1) THE great loss and injury which is being inflicted on
the British producers by the extraordinary rise in the value
of gold as compared with that of silver during the last twenty
years, consequent on changes in the laws regulating the use
of gold and silver as money in various countries.

There is nothing which has caused so much injury to
British producers of to-day comparable to the rise in the
value of gold compared to silver; but the injury already
inflicted, although very considerable, is insignificant to what
it will be unless some speedy means are found to alter the
currency system of the world. The mighty dollar—the silver
dollar I mean—is becoming almighty by its cheapness compared to gold, and unless its evil influence on British
industries is thoroughly understood by the working classes,
and its power promptly crippled, it will soon bring about
the greatest commercial revolution the world has ever
known.

The East, with its teeming millions, has, by far-seeing
minds, been looked to as the future great and permanent
market for British goods, consequently it is most necessary
that every Englishman should know what changes are taking
place, and which owe their existence entirely to cheap silver.

D

When a fixed ratio existed between gold and silver the silver dollar was worth about 4s. 2d.,and the rupee 2s. 1d., now the former is worth only 2s., and the latter 1s., or less than one-half of their original value in gold, with a tendency still to decline. Considering that the silver value of food and labour in the East has varied little within the last twenty years, and especially in the interior where the teeming millions live, it will be readily understood that the extraordinary rise in the silver price of gold has greatly diminished, and impeded the consumption of British made goods and considerably reduced their gold prices. The conservatism of the Oriental is proverbial, and it takes a great deal to make him change. But he loves money, and consequently feels the more keenly the great advance in the prices of British made goods in his own silver currency during the last twenty years.

The value of money in the East is considerable in its purchasing powers, so far as native products are concerned, and out of all proportion to what it is in England. An Oriental can buy all the necessaries of life for a few cents per day, and therefore knows and realises the value of money far more than an Englishman does. He counts the cost of everything, not only to the cent but to the tenth part of a cent. A cent is now worth less than an English farthi ng and there is a coin in everyday use all over the East one-tenth of a cent. only. This great purchasing power in general of money in the East must always be kept in mind, in order to properly understand the influence the great rise in the silver-price of gold has on the Oriental when purchasing foreign goods. To buy such goods always means the spending of a lot of money, and he only buys them as luxuries or as absolute necessities according to their nature English goods were the first introduced into the East, and they acquired a wide reputation. The Oriental once satisfied with an article always uses it if he can get it at a reasonable price. You may show him another, and it may be a better one; but he knows the old make, and will have it again and again in spite of all persuasion to the contrary. This is why so many well-known brands hold their own against new goods.

In order to explain the more clearly the changes which have and still are taking place, I will use the dollar as a unit. We will put it down as being worth, roughly, 4s., or five dollars to the pound.

As long as silver remained at a fixed ratio with gold, it was comparatively easy to do business in the East. If prices rose in gold they would naturally rise in silver; and if the Oriental could not afford to buy, he knew why, and was content to wait till prices came down again; but when silver began to fall in its ratio to gold, the silver price, or selling price in the East, of British made goods began to rise without any visible reason to the Oriental. For a time he was bewildered. To him a dollar was a dollar, and he could not see why an article which still only cost 4s. should be worth more than a dollar in silver. It was useless to try to explain it. He could not and would not understand, and rather than pay more he would do without the goods. Indeed, it is a well-known fact that for a considerable time merchants were obliged to forego their profits in order to dispose of their goods. The English manufacturer was continually advised of this, but he would not bring down his prices, and eventually the merchant had to demand more silver. Then the Oriental began to look about for cheaper goods. He did not like it at all. It was against his nature to change : he had used English goods for a long time and had got accustomed to them ; but he could not pay the increased price in his silver money, so he bought continental goods instead. The English manufacturer was duly informed of this, but he usually replied that the Oriental would soon find out his mistake;

that the continental goods were rubbish, and if once tried would never be bought again. It was the English manufacturer who had to find out his mistake; for the Oriental, once having the continental goods, made them suit his purpose, and continued to buy them because of their cheapness.

There is little doubt that the rise in the value of gold compared with silver has been the main cause of the great growth of the continental trade with the East, and that the German and Belgian iron and steel industries in particular owe most of their success to it, for once having got a footing in the market they were ever ready to undersell the British merchant in order to keep their trade.

But silver still continued to fall, and although prices in Europe fell too, their gold price did not fall in proportion to the fall in the gold value of silver, and the Oriental was again perplexed. He found the continental goods, even, too dear for his small means; but in the meantime he had studied the vexed problem of the fluctuations in the relative value of gold and silver. Food and labour cost him about the same as they had done, but British and continental goods were continually getting dearer in silver through the decline in its value as compared with that of gold, and seemed likely to continue doing so. If he could only manufacture similar goods himself, he could make plenty of money out of it, and that was what he wanted most. Pressed by necessity, and the bright prospects, he commenced, very clandestinely of course, Oriental fashion. It would not do to let anyone know; it must be kept a profound secret. They must not be known as his make, or they would not sell. They must have a foreign appearance, and be palmed off as foreign made; so he started with such as were sold by the label or wrapper. Wonderful imitations they were— the wrappers I mean—but the goods themselves positive rubbish. The primitive way in which they were produced, and the inferior materials of which they were made, could not make them otherwise; but in their foreign dress they sold, and the whole interior districts were soon flooded with them. Of course they were all British imitations, such as Bass's Beer, Guinness's Stout, Exshaw's Brandy, and even Pears' Soap, and they could all be bought in a dozen different makes, but with labels apparently perfectly genuine, and in some cases actually put up in the original bottles and wrappers. His intention, of course, was only to impose on his own countrymen, for the Oriental living in the interiors with no knowledge of European writing, deceived by the appearance of the label, would be quite satisfied with the quality of the goods. But by degrees they reached the seaports and got into European hands. In India steps were soon taken to punish the guilty, and in China the squeeze of the mandarin greatly reduced the profits. But in Japan there was no redress, there being no protection for foreign patents and trade marks; the Governments declined to interfere, and when diplomatic stress was brought to bear on them they openly encouraged it, declaring that foreigners had no right to complain; that the goods would not sell without foreign labels, and to stop the use of such labels would be to destroy the industries of Japan. Thus was inflicted upon British producers the greatest blow ever aimed at their trade in the far East. For a time the confusion was great, and the complaints severe, but, encouraged by success and supported by the Government, the Japanese set to work to improve the quality and appearance of their productions. Machinery was imported, and the best European skill obtained. Weaving, at which they were already adepts, has been greatly improved and adapted to European styles, and silks and cotton goods are largely exported to all parts of the world. Large

breweries have been built, which supply excellent beer
in quantities not only sufficient to supply the demand
of the country, but shipped largely to China and the Straits
Settlements. Dockyards have been made where the largest
ships can be built and repaired, and iron foundries and engine
shops under European supervision turn out the best of work.
A scheme is also on foot to erect large iron and steel works,
subsidised by the Government, where plates, rails, &c., can
be produced for shipbuilding and railway purposes, and so
great has been the improvement in the quality of household
requisites that European ladies who, five or six years ago
would have spurned anything Japanese made, now do most
of their shopping in the native stores, while merchants, who
for years have imported only British products and manufactures, are seeking customers all over the world for the new
goods being made in Japan.

The assistance rendered by the Japanese Government to
native manufactures and producers, not only in declining to
interfere with their using foreign patents and trade-marks,
but in many instances subsidising and fostering their industries, has made Japan the foremost manufacturing nation of
the East. But its power to compete in the markets of the
world is solely due to the cheapness of the price of silver as
compared with that of gold. Those goods which had to be
clothed in a foreign dress in order to command a sale, have
been improved, and by the use of machinery and the aid of
foreign help and experience till they can now hold their own
in their native costume. But it is to the cheapness of the
value of silver, as compared with that of gold, that they owe
their power to compete in the markets of the world.

(2) The immense temptation and inducement which this
rise in the value of gold holds out to capitalists in silver-

using countries to develop their coal mines and to erect
machinery for the purpose of supplying themselves and other
silver-using countries with the manufactured articles which
Great Britain has so long been in the habit of supplying
them with.

There is an ever-growing demand for coal in the East,
and especially by the British steamship companies trading
there. Although it exists within easy reach of most of the
ports it could not be got at a profit, and there was little
inducement to get it while a fixed ratio existed between
gold and silver which kept up the gold value of the silver
dollar. The Japanese Government tried the experiment,
and spent large sums of money in opening mines;
but they gave up the enterprise, and sold the concerns
to private companies at a great sacrifice to avoid further
loss. The gold value of the silver dollar was then worth
about 4s. Cardiff coal was used all over the East with
an occasional cargo from Australia. Its cost, with freight,
was about 40s. per ton laid down at the ports, or $10
per ton in silver. But, ten years ago, the value of the dollar
had fallen to 3s. 4d. in gold, which raised the price of coal
to $12 per ton in silver, although still costing only
40s. per ton in gold. The Japanese coal, however, could be
got for less than $10, and a few cargo steamers com-
menced to use it. It was mostly surface coal, and of inferior
quality, but as most of the freight between the Eastern ports
s earned in silver, this rise of $2 per ton in the silver
price of Cardiff coal, with no corresponding rise in the rate
of freights to meet it, was a serious matter with the steamship companies, and they began to consider the necessity of
using cheaper coal. The increased demand for Japanese
coal made its production remunerative, and capitalists were
ready to invest their capital in order to develop an industry

which offered such inducements. As the rise in the value
of gold continued so did the price of Cardiff coal increase,
while, by the aid of machinery, and an improved system of
mining, the Japanese coal got cheaper. Some of the finest
plant in the world has been laid down in Japan, the
lower seams worked, and good quality coal found
little inferior to Welsh or English. Railways have been
built to convey it to convenient ports, and mines opened all
over the country. The result is that, while the silver-price
of Cardiff coal has increased to $15 and $16 per ton in spite
of its reduced cost in gold Japanese coal of very good
quality can be bought at $3 per ton, and even less.
Consequently the British coal trade in the East has
practically ceased, and the millions of tons it would have
supplied annually had silver remained at a fixed ratio with
gold, are now procured from Japan, for all steamers trading
to the East use that fuel east of the Suez Canal.

And what has been done in the coal trade is being
attempted, and so far very successfully, with manufactured
goods, although the progress is much slower. In the former
case the demand was on the spot, and those who bought it
were well acquainted with the advantages offered, while in
the latter markets have to be found, goods sent out and
tried, and numerous changes and alterations made to suit
the varied wants. But the progress is nevertheless rapid,
and the success so encouraging that capitalists are eager to
invest their money in industries of almost every kind.
Twenty years ago any connection with trade was considered
degrading in the eyes of the Japanese, and no respectable
person would have anything to do with it. The very lowest
only were in it, and they were looked on as beings contaminated
by some loathsome disease. To-day it is the "El Dorado"
of the highest and most intelligent. What can have brought
about the change, except the profits already derived, and

now eagerly sought for in the manufacture of goods which hitherto had been purchased from Great Britain and the Continent.

A comparison of the relative values of gold and silver twenty years ago with those of to-day will the better enable us to understand the positions of the producers of Great Britain and Japan at the present time. The original value of £1 sterling was about $5 in silver, the value at the present time of £1 sterling is about $10 in silver, so that if British goods cost the same to produce now as they did twenty years ago they would be worth just double the amount in silver.

The original value of the dollar was 4s., or say $5 to the pound sterling, now the value of the dollar is only 2s., or say $10 to the pound sterling, so that supposing it costs the same to produce goods in the East now as it did twenty years ago, they can be sold for half the amount in gold.

The result is that goods produced in gold-using countries have become double their price in silver, and those produced in silver-using countries reduced to half their price in gold. The effect requires no explanation. It is argued that the cheap produce from the East, such as sugar, rice, grain, tea &c., enables the British producer to live cheaper, and consequently produce cheaper. This is good so far as it goes, but it cannot possibly go far enough to enable him to compete with the cheap Eastern labour. If he could produce at half the gold price he did twenty years ago he would still be only on a level with the Oriental. The fact is that goods produced in gold-using countries are dear in silver-using countries and are the less in demand, while those produced in silver-using countries are cheap in gold-using countries, and their consumption is continually increasing. The result is that in the former trade is declining and unprofitable, with plenty of cheap money lying idle; in the latter, trade is plentiful and profitable, capital scarce and dividends large.

It will be seen that the result of this rise in the value of gold has almost invariably meant a rise in the silver value of British manufactures. I know of no British industry which has been able to so economise in its methods of production as to be able to regularly supply its goods to Eastern countries at fixed silver prices. If such should exist, I can positively assert that no rival enterprise has been started against it unless possibly it may be something specially required for Government use, which would be difficult to get in times of war, and is made at a greater cost than it could be imported to insure its possession at all times.

(3) That in the competitive manufacturing industries of the world the divergence of value between gold and silver must inevitably lead to the substitution of the cheap labour of silver-using countries for the more highly paid labour of gold-using ones—a substitution which is already taking place, and, unless some international agreement be come to at once, must lead to the ruin of many British industries, and the throwing out of employment of tens of thousands of workpeople.

If one man were as good as another, under the same conditions and in the same field, the one who could do the work cheapest would generally get the most of it to do. Such is Nature's law, and, unless impeded, soon works out its own end, just as water finds its own level. The invention of steam and its application of machinery gave the British producer an advantage, and he was not slow to turn it to good account and build up for himself the first position among the manufacturing countries of the world. Cobden tried by his system of free trade to permanently secure to the British nation this position. If other countries would follow suit, so

much the better, for the cheaper British goods could be sold
so much greater would be the demand for them, while cheap
produce was the very thing she wanted to enable her to
cheapen her production. Nothing could have been better;
but other countries would not take the bait. They could not
compete successfully with British goods; so after England
had adopted free trade, instead of following suit as Cobden
had expected they would, they turned round and increased
their duties in order to protect and foster their industries.
This was not an unmixed blessing to them, for it raised the
prices of their imports without in any way diminishing those
of their exports. It, however, seriously hampered British
trade and considerably diminished the growth of it.

But in the East the results are entirely different. There
are no duties of serious consideration, and they could not
be increased at will; in fact, there were no industries to
protect, and consequently no necessity to increase them.
The great thing was to get British goods as cheap as they
could. But the continual rise in the value of gold, as
compared with that of silver, has changed everything.
British goods got so dear in their silver value that the
Oriental was forced to make for himself, and the decline
in the value of the white metal has so helped him in his
work that he can not only make sufficient for himself but is
able to export them to advantage. The rise in the value of
gold has doubled the silver price of British goods in the
East, and has made their use almost prohibitive, while the
fall in the value of silver has brought down by over a half
the gold price of Oriental goods in gold-using countries, and
is continually increasing the demand for them. The
conditions are so unequal that it seems impossible to continue
the struggle long. It is like handicapping the champion by
giving to his opponent half the distance of the race.

The impossibility of the European competing with the

Oriental in the open field has been proved in America. The Chinese there by their low wages so monopolised labour that they had to be excluded from the country or the European workmen would have starved or been driven out. But the European countries are not threatened with the labourer himself (as the Americans were, where he knew the price of European labour, and could learn, understand, how much he should get himself), but with the products of that labour done at Oriental wages. Besides, it would be easy enough to refuse to employ an Oriental to do your work while it is difficult to decline to buy goods made by him, especially as they improve in quality and get cheaper in price. The temptation to buy them becomes all the greater as the money earned by the British workmen get less. He is the more prone to do so, and declines to buy his own made but dearer goods. Protective countries are better off. They can impose increased duties on Oriental goods, and so stop them from flooding their markets. But England with her free trade has no defence, and the brunt of the burden will fall upon her workmen. The evil is getting greater. Every farthing in the increase of the price of gold as compared with that of silver makes British goods 1 per cent. dearer in the East, while every farthing decrease in the price of silver makes Oriental goods 1 per cent. cheaper in gold-using countries. These new industries are growing very rapidly in Japan, and what is being done there can and will be done in China, India, and other places. Once well established the Oriental will hold on to them in spite of all opposition, and unless some speedy remedy is found to alter the currency system of the world their products will be spread broadcast all over the world to the ruin of British industries and untold disaster to thousands and thousands of workmen.   THOMAS HOLYOAKE BOX.

YOKOHAMA, *August* 21, 1894.

P.S.—Since writing this paper a new Treaty has been published, made between Great Britain and Japan, by which the latter country will be allowed to increase its duties on British products to the extent of 10 per cent., after five years from the date of the Treaty. This will be a further blow to British commerce and the working man.

THE FALL IN SILVER

AND ITS

EFFECT ON BRITISH TRADE.

———

BY
DAVID OCTAVIUS CROAL,
LONDON.

———

THE FALL IN SILVER AND ITS EFFECT ON BRITISH TRADE.

BY

DAVID OCTAVIUS CROAL.

In the later days of September this year a gentleman of some authority as a financial writer suggested to a mercantile audience interested in Eastern trade that in supporting a reform of the monetary standard they were on the wrong tack. "Instead of reasoning," he remarked, "from currency to commerce, which in nine cases out of ten became mere metaphysics, let them reason from commerce to currency, which would be business." The challenge was daring and hardly judicious, coming as it did from a supporter of the existing monetary status. As a rule, the advocates of the existing system prefer to avoid the commercial side of the question—for reasons that are obvious. They content themselves with the argument, or rather the assumption, that British interests must suffer through a change in standards because the value of our capital invested abroad, and the return obtained from it, must be depreciated. The commercial side of the picture they studiously neglect. It is highly desirable that we should obtain the biggest possible return from our foreign investments—provided we do not break our debtors by making honest fulfilment of their obligations too onerous; but it is equally desirable, indeed

E

more so, that the capital actively employed in industry should not be permitted to become less remunerative through the change in monetary conditions that has been going on during the past quarter of a century. It is the purpose of this paper to inquire whether the dislocation of monetary standards can be proved to have been detrimental to British industry and trade; and, if that be established, to discover to what extent our interests have suffered, and how far losses already sustained may be irremediable. It need hardly be said that, enormous as is our stake as a creditor country, it is of less importance than our industrial and commercial interests. Capital invested in home or foreign funds is passive, whereas money employed in manufactures is reproductive, creating work and wages, furnishing freight to railways and steamboats, and generally bringing prosperity in its train. If then, in determining whether or not a change in monetary policy should be made, we had to choose between slightly infringing on the interests of funded capital or sacrificing those of our industrial organism, there could be little doubt in which direction the scale should turn.

Reference has been made to the neglect of the trade aspect of the monetary problem by the single standard men, but the reformers must also bear some share of responsibility for refraining from placing this side of the question before the public. It is true that the Lancashire movement in favour of Bimetallism is inspired by a bitter experience of the evils which the dislocation of the world's standards has brought on the cotton industry. Lancashire has been convinced by the resistless logic of the emptying pocket, but the inert mass of public opinion must be stirred by the presentation of clear and tangible proofs of the injury that has already been done to the national trade by the fall in silver. Five-sixths of the intelligent population of the country do not understand the simple principles which account for the detrimental influence of falling and irregular exchanges on our foreign trade. Yet these principles have less in common with abstruse economical science than with every-day common sense. It stands to reason that if in India a rupee, in China a tael, in Mexico and Central and South America a dollar, to-day buys as much rice or wheat, or other necessity, as in time past the natives of these countries will expect these coins to buy as much cloth or similar goods, and will resent having to pay more for them. Moreover, as in these countries wages remain virtually unchanged, the inhabitants are actually not in possession of greater wealth to spend on such articles. It follows equally that if an importer of foreign goods into such countries can nowadays only realise about half as much as formerly for the rupee, the tael, or the dollar in the currency in which he calculates, and in which the cost of producing the goods is paid, he must either abandon the business, submit to have his profits pruned to vanishing point, or take steps to secure a complete re-adjustment of the terms on which the goods are made and sold.

Since the fall in silver began over twenty years ago, the gold-basis manufacturer, dealing with silver countries, has been trying hard to adopt the last alternative as a means of avoiding the second and postponing the first, with a wonderful degree of success. Circumstances have helped him up to a certain point. Money has become less valuable, and so he has been able to borrow capital at rather easier rates. Communication and transit are more rapid and less expensive. Machinery has been improved and the potentialities of cheaper productions have consequently been increased. All these factors have combined to make it possible up to a certain point to bring prices of manufactured goods within reach of the purchasing power of silver-using consumers. So long as the decline in

E2

silver was gradual the gold-basis manufacturer suffered only moderately, his enterprise and resolution enabling him to recoup himself by economies in production, by modifying his views of fair profits, and by reducing his standard of living. But when, through the action of some Governments and the inaction of others, silver began to fall by pence where before it had fallen by fractions, the limit of readjustment was reached. It cannot be denied that the position of the cotton industry—which has the biggest and most direct stake in our trade with silver countries—is exceedingly precarious. The situation and the attitude of the Lancashire manufacturer were clearly set forth by Mr. William Taylor, of Blackburn, at the recent Bimetallic Conference in London. "The difficulty that presented itself," he said, "was this—that a fall in the exchange from 1s. 3d. to 1s. 1½d. caused a loss of 6d. per piece of cloth worth 5s. Who had to lose the 6d.? The fight for the 6d. went on until it was adjusted, and in his experience it always ended in the manufacturer getting the worst of it. Why? Because the buyer could wait and the manufacturer could not, except by stopping his mill, thereby throwing his work-people out of employment. Before he would do that, he would submit to considerable loss, in the hope that trade might soon improve." Having thus stated generally how the fall in silver tends to injure our great industries, it will be well to endeavour to give concrete examples from actual experience, and to show to what extent our interests have already suffered.

It is to China that we must look for the most cogent example of the injury done to British trade by the fall in silver. It is the custom of those who preach the infallibility of the single gold standard to explain the decline in the profitable character of our commerce with silver countries by reference to the improved means of transit and communication, and

other social and economic changes, that have been pro-
ceeding coincidently with the depreciation of silver. But in
China there has been no appreciable alteration in social
habits or economic conditions during the last quarter of a
century. That is one reason why China affords so suitable
a ground for working out the point under discussion. But
there is an even stronger reason. Thanks to the well directed
diligence of Mr. Jamieson, British Consul at Shanghai, it
has been proved, as effectually as precise and careful figures
can prove anything, that the purchasing price of silver in
relation to commodities of native origin has hardly varied
within the last twenty years. This is a matter of first-rate
importance to the present inquiry. It establishes that the
Chinese find that the tael of silver purchases to-day practically
the same quantity of native produce as it has always done in
their experience. Thus, nothing has occurred to reconcile
them to an alteration in the price of the few staples of foreign
manufacture which they use freely. It implies that if the
foreign producer desires to retain Chinese custom he must
endeavour to bring his goods into the market at or about the
same figure as he did before silver fell. The Chinaman
expects to-day as much for the tael as he did twenty years
ago, but the tael he paid then was worth 6s. 8d. to the seller,
whereas it is now worth less than half that amount in gold.

As a matter of fact, until very recently indeed, the silver
price of foreign commodities tended to decline in China. A
piece of grey shirtings which in 1870-4 brought 1·48
Haikwan taels, in 1892 brought only 1·01, so that the
producer had not only to face the fall in the exchange value
of the money received for his goods, but had to be satisfied
with a reduced sum in the depreciated currency. Consul
Jamieson, whose information is drawn from " Chamber of
Commerce price lists and other contemporaneous market
reports," points out that until last year the Manchester

prices of cotton goods such as are most used in China fell almost *pari passu* with the decline in silver. " An ordinary piece of shirtings," he writes, " which in 1872-4 cost from 10s. to 10s. 6d. in Manchester, is now invoiced out at 6s. to 6s. 2d." From figures of actual sales at Shanghai he shows that medium shirtings selling at 1·72 Shanghai taels in 1888, sold at 1·70 in January last year. Shortly afterwards prices began to rise, the idea being that Lancashire merchants were stimulated to raise their lists by the steadier value of the rupee. By December the same shirtings had risen to 2·12 taels, and the result is apparent in the diminished purchases of cotton pieces in China last year. From the British Consular reports from sixteen of the principal treaty ports I find that the imports of white and grey shirtings and T. cloths fell from 16,459,174 pieces in 1892 to 11.121.585 in 1893. These figures do not cover the entire trade of China, and Mr. Kopsch, Statistical Secretary of the Imperial Maritime Customs, gives the diminution in these three leading articles as 3,175,000 pieces. Mr. Kopsch's statistics exclude imports from silver-using countries, and so we may take them as fairly representing the loss sustained by gold-basis manufacturers in China in a single year. That loss is sensational enough, and it seems to show beyond doubt that if English manufacturers desire to maintain their trade with China at its old magnitude in point of bulk they must be content with a smaller return in point of money. Directly they attempt to obtain better prices down drops the quantity of goods sold. To all appearance the attempt to force up prices has failed, if we are to judge by the values in the Board of Trade returns for the first half of this year. In the six months China took from us 254,954,100 yards of cotton piece goods of all descriptions, of a total value of £2,357,753 which works out at an average of 2·21 pence per yard. In the corresponding half of 1893 a similar calculation gives the average value at 2·50 pence per yard. The difference of roughly a farthing per yard was equivalent on the 255 million yards to over £265,570. It would be a mistake to lay much stress on figures obtained by lumping together all classes of cotton pieces in this way, but, making all due allowance for the rough and ready method, the result is certainly a striking illustration of the sacrifices which a leading industry has to undergo in maintaining its hold in Chinese markets.

But it may be asked, is it certain that the contraction in the importation of European, chiefly English, goods into China is due to the fall in exchange? In reply, I will cite the evidence of a number of our Consuls whose reports are virtually unanimous. But, first, it may be well to quote a pointed passage from the 1893 report of Mr. Kopsch, of the Imperial Chinese Customs, of whose figures I have already made use. Mr. Kopsch writes: "To the observer in the East it seems inexplicable that the gold-currency countries, while striving to extend their trade, should resolutely ignore the fact, so clearly demonstrated by the decline in the demand for piece goods, that to the millions in China the tael or ounce of silver is still a tael of undiminished purchasing power, whether the sterling value be 6s. or 3s., and that so soon as the discredited tael fails to buy the same quantity of foreign goods as heretofore the consumer ceases to be a customer, and will supply his own wants by manufacturing textiles from home-grown materials." To the point raised in the last clause I shall return later, meantime it is enough to say that Mr. Kopsch speaks with authority. Consul Warren, of Hankow, attributes the " sudden collapse " of cotton imports almost entirely to "the steady fall in exchange, native dealers refusing to give the higher prices which importers were obliged to ask." Consul Allen testifies from Chefoo that the English manufacturer "cannot afford to sell at the rate in silver which used to pay him a profit, and the Chinese customer cannot afford to buy as much as he did, and so trade must diminish." Consul Mansfield of Foochow opines that "the fall in silver will, if it continues, speedily handicap Manchester out of the market." Such quotations might be multiplied indefinitely, for each Consul reiterates the same opinion in some shape or form. Many of them refer to the extent to which native and Japanese competition is ousting English goods, but that is a department of the inquiry which will be dealt with separately. The opinion of trained observers on the spot—men who have no interest in misrepresenting facts and tendencies, and whose reports are made to a Government which has little desire to be put in possession of such unpalatable truths—is unanimously that British goods are losing ground in China solely because of the fall in exchange. But, it may be triumphantly asked by a single standard critic, how comes it that in the first six months of 1894, the exports of cotton piece goods to China, were greater than in the first half of 1893 ? That is a troublesome question to deal with. If I reply that the comparison is affected by the strike in Lancashire, early in 1893, the critic would claim that the same fact vitiated any conclusions I might draw from a decrease in 1893 as compared with 1892. So it would if I were arguing solely from these figures, and not in the light of disinterested expert testimony from China. And at best the critic would score little, for the larger exports simply illustrate the determination of our manufacturers to hold the field as long as they can, even at a loss. I have shown by calculations, based on the Board of Trade figures, that the value of these exports has fallen though the quantities have increased, a clear proof that the trade is less profitable—in other words, that our manufacturers are suffering losses.

In all other silver countries, British manufacturers are meeting the same obstacles as in China. In Japan there was a decrease of £1,302,920 in the value of British imports in 1891 ; in 1892 the decrease was £225,103, and the separate reports of the various Consuls show that in 1893 the same tendency was visible. At the same time the imports of the country in general increased, all the growth being in goods from other silver countries. Mr. Spring Rice, of the Tokio Legation, points out that in 1892 English manufacturers received the same return in sterling for 118 yards of piece goods as they did for 108 yards in 1890, a very appreciable loss. Consul Troup, of Yokohama, writing in May last, says, "Since the further fall in exchange, which has taken place since the close of last year, the import trade in manufactures has been stagnant, and to what extent the Japanese consumer will be prepared to rise to the advanced dollar price of imports is not yet evident. To say the least, the trade in imports seems likely to suffer great restrictions, and, in the case of articles which come into competition with home Japanese manufactures, probable extinction." At several of the Japanese ports the arrivals of English cotton cloths have dwindled to nothing. Similar reports come from Corea, in which our trade interest is now quite microscopic, though it was of some value before the fall in silver shut us out of the market. From other Eastern countries we receive the same story. Reporting on the trade of the Straits Settlements in 1892, the Governor referred to the reduction in the imports of cotton pieces, and of European goods generally, as due to the decline in exchange. Our Consuls in Siam repeat the tale. Acting-Consul Joly, at Macao, attributes the decrease in imports from England to the fall in silver. The people in Macao are poor and must have cheap goods, and ours are beyond their pocket. Hence they have turned first to cheap German stuffs and still more to Japanese manufactures.

Leaving Asia for Central and South America we encounter

precisely similar evidence. Unfortunately, the statistics of
imports are not so careful, trustworthy, or up to date as those
in China, but our Consuls do their best to make up for
the shortcomings of native officials. From Mexico,
Mr. Lional Carden some time ago sent an exhaustive
report on the effect of the fall in silver, in which he
dwelt on the increasing cost of foreign goods in the native
currency, giving elaborate tables which showed how the
purchasing power of the population is curtailed at each fall
in the value of the dollar. Consul Chapman, at Vera Cruz,
testifies to the decline of British trade, and expresses a belief
that it must go on diminishing unless some change speedily
takes place in the monetary conditions. He illustrates how
importing houses, while obtaining bigger prices in silver,
suffered "an actual loss when the profit has to be accounted
for in gold." In Costa Rica we find the dollar value of
English goods rising while the sterling yield is diminishing.
From Guatemala and Venezuela our Consuls send similar wails
over the decay of British trade, and in fact the experience is
universal in countries on a silver basis, countries many of
them only half developed and partially exploited—the very
markets in which we should have expected our commercial
dealings to expand as years went on, but for this in-
superable obstacle of exchange, which is a greater bar
to trade than the most comprehensive and onerous tariffs,
for it knows no free list. A glance through the figures
of our exports to silver countries in the last ten years, as
given in the *Statistical Abstract* of the United Kingdom just
published, will show to the most casual observer how
infinitely more profitable our trade with them was in 1890
and 1891, the two most recent years of high silver, than in
any immediately before or after.

That British manufacturers and exporters are not only
losing money from the fall in silver, but are actually losing

established markets, seems undeniable in the light of the
figures already cited. It falls now to examine how far we
are being supplanted in silver-using countries; in other words,
how far our loss of trade is likely to be permanent. It is
well known that the cotton spinning and weaving industries
of Bombay were brought into existence and fostered by the
fall in silver. Wages were paid in silver, and thus the cost
of production was so much smaller that Bombay yarn
became a dangerous competitor with the Lancashire article
in all Eastern markets. To-day, in turn, the Bombay manufacturers find serious rivals in the cotton mills of Japan
and China. It does not form part of the present inquiry
to consider the effect on Bombay of the separation effected
in June, 1893, between the value of the rupee and that of
silver; but there is abundant evidence, both in the Indian
trade and navigation returns, and in the reports from China,
that the change was inimical to trade between the two.
"The dislocation in exchange," writes Mr. Kopsch in his
valuable report on the Chinese trade of last year, "brought
about by according a fictitious value to the rupee, and
closing the Indian Mints to the coinage of silver, has
resulted, as predicted, in a very serious falling off in the
entire trade from India to China." This is germane to the
particular subject now under review, for it illustrates how
immediate is the effect on commerce of a breach between the
monetary standards of two countries. Japan has been the
first of far Eastern countries to see that with silver-paid
labour it is easy to compete with the products of Western
industry. Consul Enslie, of Hiogo, remarks: "One phase
of English industries with regard to the far East, inevitable
but intensely interesting, and of the most vital importance
is, that for some years past, the importers of the manufactured articles and those of the manufacturing machinery
have been competing, side by side, much to the steadily

increasing detriment of the former. This reference is, of course, meant to apply to cotton yarn and cotton spinning machinery."

Our Consul at Yokohama notes the same phenomenon of English machinery arriving to enable the Japanese to compete with English cottons and other articles. Consul Enslie shows that in 1883 Japan's imports of raw cotton were only 2,808,318 lb. whereas in 1893 they were 154,442,368 lb. Mr. De Bunsen, Secretary to the British Legation in Tokio, in reporting on Japanese trade of 1892 drew the attention of the Foreign Secretary to "the alteration which has taken place in the trade of Japan in the last few years, owing to the progress of Japanese industries. The imports of raw material are increasing at the expense of the imports of manufactured goods. While the sterling value of the imports has increased 19 per cent. since 1887, the value of the import of cotton yarn and piece goods has decreased 17 per cent., the value of the import of woollen goods is stationary. On the other hand, Japan imported last year eleven times the quantity of raw cotton imported in 1887, and since the same year her export of fabrics manufactured in Japan has increased nearly four hundred per cent. In the far East, Japan has now become a competitor with England in certain lines of cotton goods." The competition of Japanese goods has also, according to the same authority, reacted on the imports of woollens which are decreasing. In the 1892 Consular Report from Hiogo particulars were given of twenty-one cotton mills, only three of which paid dividends of less than 12 per cent. (none below 8 per cent.), while ten of them paid over 20 per cent. The 1893 report shows that two of the mills which only paid 8 and 9 per cent. in 1892, had improved their profits to 10 and 12½ per cent. respectively. Nor do the Japanese confine their rivalry with Europeans to cotton, much of which goes to China to

compete with us. They have successfully introduced the manufacture of beer, gunpowder, saddlery, cement, matches,
printing paper, soap, bricks and leather, besides minor sundries, with the result that imports of these articles from
Europe have practically died out. And they are supplying
goods of these classes to all the neighbouring silver countries.
The latest Consular Reports also indicate that Japan will
soon be independent of foreign iron and sugar. Not only
that, but it is mentioned by our Consul, at Ningpo, that the
machinery used for cleaning and ginning raw cotton there
is supplied by the Japanese. From Macao we learn that
cheap Japanese imitations of European goods of all sorts
flood the bazaars.

Even sleepy, unenterprising China has awakened to the
fact that she can successfully and profitably make her own
cotton yarn and cloth. The building of mills has been kept
back through the extreme caution of the Chinese. They fear
that a recovery in silver might rob them of their advantage
in the native market, and might enable later competitors
to buy European machinery more cheaply, and so cut the
pioneers out. The lowness of exchange has thus helped us by
retarding Chinese investments in machinery. But in 1892 two
mills were in full operation in Shanghai, one confining itself to
the manufacture of yarn, the other both spinning and weaving.
The first employed 15,000 spindles and turned out 2,000,000 lb.
of yarn in 1892, the second employed 25,000 spindles and
550 looms, producing in 1892 a million pounds of yarn and four
million yards of drills and sheetings. This mill was burned
in October, 1893, but rebuilding was begun at once, and the
new machinery includes 100,000 spindles and 1,500 looms.
Other three mills are in course of construction, and by the
end of this year Shanghai is expected to have 150,000
spindles running. In April, 1893, a mill of 700 looms was
opened at Hankow, and a spinning mill is being erected, the

machinery having already arrived from England. Particulars of the output of the factory are not obtainable. But our Consuls at various ports note a striking increase in the arrivals of native cloth, most notable in 1892, for the burning of the Shanghai mill made a big difference last year. At Ningpo a cotton mill opened in 1892 earned an acknowledged profit of $10,000 last year, and our Consul thinks this is greatly understated. A spinning mill is now nearing completion at Ningpo. Even at Chungking, right in the interior, a project is on foot for the establishment of a cotton mill, and the capital had been largely subscribed at the date of the latest Consular Report. Like the Japanese, the Chinese have also turned their attention to the manufacture of Portland cement, and a well-equipped mill has been for several years at work near Tientsin, with which it is connected by railway, and a factory in the same own supplies local requirements in the way of matches, which formerly were imported. These straws show which way the wind is blowing, and it has set in a direction that bodes no good to English manufacturers but much permanent injury.

Mexico is doing precisely the same as Japan and China. At Orizaba, in the State of Vera Cruz, " will be found some of the finest English-made machinery ; and cotton prints are now turned out as good as, if not superior to, the imported article. The production of these mills has been affected by the great difference in exchange ; sales have increased considerably during the last three years, whilst profits have been very fair. Some of the shares of cotton factories in Mexico are at from 60 to 80 per cent. premium." So writes our Consul at Vera Cruz, and he further points out that though at first these mills used imported raw cotton almost exclusively, " the fall in silver has caused more attention to be given to this article, and the factories at Orizaba are now

using home-grown cotton as much as possible." A jute
factory is on the point of being opened at Orizaba. The
Mexican Financier of a recent date, in announcing the
inauguration of a new factory, remarked : " Just as Europe
is forcing the Orientals to manufacture for themselves by the
anti-silver policy now favoured there, so here on this continent the silver-using countries are being forced to make
everything possible for themselves. What do we see in
Mexico to-day, but a well-marked movement in the direction
of a home supply of many articles of prime necessity—in
paper, textiles, soap, iron goods, &c. The combination of
Governments and great bankers against silver is certain,
ultimately, if persisted in, greatly to injure the business
of the manufacturers of Europe. The silver standard
nations will keep more of their money at home." It is
needless to multiply examples further, for no one with
the slighest regard for facts can deny that new industries,
fostered by the bonus which a depreciated currency
gives to home manufacturers, are springing up in all the
silver countries. In the meantime they are only partially
satisfying the needs of their own compatriots, but before
long they will not only be able to supply their own native
markets but those of their neighbours. Quite a new inter-
change trade is springing up between the silver countries.
The cultivation of raw cotton is making great strides in
China, much of it being shipped to Japan, whence some returns in the shape of piece goods. Japan is not only
sending cottons and sundries of all sorts to the silver peoples
in far Eastern seas, but it is supplying machinery and im-
plements to some portions of China, and to Corea, as our Consular Reports show. We have seen how profitable are the cotton
factories of Japan, of China and of Mexico—their dividends
high ; their shares at substantial premiums. Compare this
with the unhappy state of cotton companies in Lancashire.

I have referred to a dozen reports issued in one day at the end of June showing the position of as many spinning companies in and near Oldham. Of these ten showed an adverse balance, and only two were able to pay dividends. This is unfortunately a fair representation of the state of the cotton industry in Lancashire—an industry giving employment to hundreds of thousands of people, and furnishing a very large proportion of our entire foreign trade.

Many attempts are made to prove that the contraction of our trade with silver countries, and the extension of manufactures there, have little or nothing to do with the depreciation in silver. A few months ago Dr. Giffen, of the Board of Trade, compiled a report on the progress of the foreign trade of the United Kingdom in recent years. There he showed that in 1884-5 goods from this country constituted 25 per cent. of the whole imports of China, whereas in 1890-1-2 our proportion fell to 21 per cent. In the case of Japan the fall was from 45 to 34 per cent. It was agreeable to discover that we had not lost ground to our European competitors in these markets, but there were other features less welcome. "It should be remarked," wrote Dr. Giffen, "that the chief increase in the relative proportion of the imports into Japan has gone to the Corea, to India, and to other minor countries which are geographically much nearer than ourselves." This explanation struck Dr. Giffen as so happy and forcible that he repeated it. But it may fairly be asked if these other countries have in the last seven years become geographically nearer Japan than they were before? If there has been a change in the distribution of Eastern trade, we should surely look for an explanation to those conditions which have altered and not to those which are immutable. It is childish to assume that Eastern peoples have only awakened within the last few years to the consciousness that they are nearer one another than to Europe. What they have become alive to is the existence of the barrier of exchange between them and Europe. If Dr. Giffen's ingenuous principle were carried to its legitimate conclusion, it would follow that the reduction in trade between India and Japan during the last fifteen months was due to an enlargement of the geographical distance between them, and not to the creation of a new monetary standard in India. The immediate shrinkage in Indian exports to China and Japan which followed the monetary change of June, 1893—to which the Indian trade returns and the Consular Reports from the far East bear concurrent testimony—affords unequivocal proof that commerce is more rapidly and seriously influenced by exchange than by tariffs or " geographical " situation. Yet while our industries are languishing and our exports contracting, the official statisticians entertain us with the shibboleths of an effete and exploded school of economic thought. It is no pleasure to any one to dwell on the decay of British commerce with any portion of the globe, but it is a duty to recognise facts, however hard, to endeavour to ascertain the causes, and if possible to prescribe a remedy. So long as we are content to accept the fallacy that geography and distance are the determining factors in the distribution of trade between nations we shall have to go on deploring the steady decadence of our commercial pre-eminence, perhaps even of our industrial existence.

The scheme of this paper requires that the disastrous effect on our trade of the fall in silver should be examined from two points of view : (a) when there has been, through the appreciation of gold, a rise in the silver price of our goods; and (b) when there has been a fall in the gold price of them. It is rather difficult to maintain the distinction between the two sets of circumstances ; but examples of both have been given in the course of this paper. I have produced evidence from Chinese reports and statistics to show

F

that when in 1893 Lancashire exporters endeavoured to
raise their price lists, the consumption of their manufactures
at once declined. The evidence from Mexico is to precisely
the same effect. The Board of Trade returns for the first
six months of the present year confirm the view of our
Consuls. In the first six months of 1892 the average value
of cotton piece goods, shipped to Mexico, was 2·65 pence
per yard, and the exports were fairly large. In 1893 the
average value rose fractionally to 2·67 pence per yard, and
there was a decrease of three million yards in the shipments
to Mexico. In the first half of this year the average value
per yard at export had fallen to 2·50 pence, and the shipments
rose 2½ million yards. Thus, whenever the gold price was
raised, and consequently the silver equivalent, there was a
sharp decline in our cotton piece goods trade with Mexico;
whenever Lancashire conceded lower prices a recovery took
place. I have already given the result of similar calculations in
the case of China. The same characteristic may be observed in
our shipments of cotton yarn. In the first half of 1892 the
value of yarn sent to Bombay was 9·89 pence per pound. A
year later it rose to 10·50 pence, and the shipments were less
than half. This year the price has fallen again to 9·61 pence,
and a considerable recovery occurred in the volume of
trade, though the 1892 level was not attained. In the case
of the Straits Settlements precisely the same thing occurred.
In 1893 the price rose to 11·15 pence from 10·59 pence
in 1892, and the shipments of yarn fell to less than half
of the former volume. This year the average price has
fallen again to 9·42 pence per pound and the exports have
exceeded the 1892 figure. These are merely representa-
tive instances, the selection of them being distributed
over India, the Straits, China and Mexico to show the
universality of the experience. If a diminished volume
of exports coincident with an advance in price and an

improvement in shipments concurrent with a fall in price do not indicate the direct operation of cause and effect, it would be hard to discover what else they do illustrate. It seems clearly demonstrated that a rise in the silver price of English goods in silver countries at once reduces the consumption and stimulates the efforts of their populations to provide similar manufactures for themselves. A reduction in the gold price, made in order to secure our hold on markets slipping from our grasp, means an enormous diminution in the remunerative character of our trade. I have already pointed out that had the piece goods shipped to China in the first six months of this year been invoiced at the prices current in the same period of 1893, the result would have been an increase in the sterling return of £265,000, or over 11 per cent. on goods valued for export at £2,357,750. The argument from commerce to currency which the Bimetallists are challenged to take up does not tell in favour of the maintenance of the existing monetary standards.

No attempt has been made in this paper to run through the whole gamut of British trade and industry so as to show to what extent individual manufacturing interests have been injured through the fall in silver. What is true of the cotton trade is true of all others, though as our exports of miscellaneous. goods to silver countries are too small to be separately specified in Board of Trade returns, or other authoritative publications, it is not so easy to detect and exhibit the restrictive influence on our outward commerce of falling exchanges. We have seen that Japan is supplying hardware as well as textiles to herself and her neighbours. Japanese coal competes, even on the Pacific coast of South America, not only with coal from Cardiff but with shipments from New South Wales. The Indian coalfields have been developed to such an extent that Welsh fuel has almost disappeared from Calcutta. No doubt the construction of railways has helped towards this, but if the Indian coal were not dug by miners paid in silver it could not even now be laid down in Calcutta on terms to compete with Cardiff, due allowance being made for the superior steam-raising qualities of the latter which enables it to command a better price than the indigenous product. In the train of coal, manufacturing industries are always to be found. Consul Enslie, of Tokio, gives interesting particulars regarding the experimental production of iron in Japan, and hints that the country, which now imports much iron, may become self-supporting in that respect. When the Eastern markets for coal, iron, and cotton, are being gradually filched from us, not so much by the superior enterprise of our rivals, but by the insidious influence of a monetary revolution, it behoves us to reconsider our position. It may be said that English investors must not be made to suffer because Lancashire and Yorkshire desire to maintain their profits. But profits have already almost disappeared from the cotton spinning and weaving industries, and the wages fund is being trenched upon. There is no difference of opinion between operatives and employers in Lancashire as to the impossibility of improving wages, and it is doubtful if they can even be maintained at their present level. The country has already experienced what a starving Lancashire means, and memory must be short indeed if the recollection of the cotton famine has died out. No one in those days would have ventured to say that the woe of Lancashire was not a national question. The loss inflicted on our trade by the fall in silver is not confined to the County Palatine, but even if it were, the urgent necessity for action could not be gainsaid. Governments have admitted that the sufferings of officials from the fall in the rupee demanded redress; can they remain much longer deaf to the appeal of a shrinking commerce, or indifferent to the threatening ruin of industries that employ millions of British capital and bring bread to thousands of British mouths?

DAVID OCTAVIUS CROAL.

SEQUEL

BY

SIR HENRY MEYSEY-THOMPSON.

SEQUEL

BY

SIR HENRY MEYSEY-THOMPSON.

———

Now, having read these papers, I hope we have all made up our minds—

(1) That we *do* wish the home and principal seat of the great manufacturing industries of the world—the cotton, woollen, worsted, linen, jute, iron and steel, machinery, glass, pottery, leather, clothing, and many others—should continue to be in the United Kingdom, as hitherto, and that they should be carried on by English, Scotch, Irish, and Welsh workmen; and we do *not* wish to see them banished to the soil of India, China, Japan, and Mexico, and carried on by Indian, Chinese, Japanese, and Mexican workmen.

(2) That, at this present actual moment, work is being done by Indian, Chinese, Japanese, and Mexican workmen, which would have been at this present actual moment in the hands of English, Scotch, Irish, and Welsh workmen, if the divergence of value between silver and gold had not taken place, or if the English Government did not obstinately oppose any reform of the present monetary laws.

(3) That it is certain that our present monometallic policy must tend to drive these industries away from the soil of the United Kingdom, and cause them to be carried on, instead, on the soil of India, China, and Japan.

Now, as the banishment of these manufacturing industries would be a tremendous loss to England and other gold-using countries, let us see if we can find any advantage which they gain by the present system sufficient to compensate them for this loss.

Let us take first the case of the other gold-using countries of Europe, which are mostly what are called debtor-countries. It seems to me that they are almost entirely losers by the present monetary system, and that the attitude of these countries towards the question would seem absolutely incomprehensible to any one who lost sight of the fact that the interests of peoples and of Governments are not always identical.

Here you have States owing large sums of money in the form of National Debts, on which interest has to be paid annually in gold. Every producer in the country has to lay aside every year a certain portion of what he produces, in order to pay his share of the interest on the debt. How much of his produce he has to lay aside depends upon price, that is to say, on whether gold is plentiful and cheap, or scarce and dear. If plentiful and cheap, he has to give little produce; if scarce and dear, he has to give a great deal.

Now if these countries had had, instead of paying gold to their creditors, to pay an annual tribute of so many tons of lead to one country, let us suppose England, the situation would then have been grasped at once. Everyone would have seen at once that the proportion of his produce which he would have to give annually to buy his share of the lead would depend on whether lead was plentiful and cheap, or scarce and dear, and the supply of lead in the world would have become at once a source of interest to every taxpayer. Governments would have been urged to offer rewards for the

discovery of new sources of lead-supply, and to give sub-
ventions to lead-miners. Anyone who discovered a substitute
for the use of lead would be looked upon as a public bene-
factor, while anyone who wasted lead unnecessarily would be
looked upon as an enemy to his country.

Yet, though abundance or scarcity of the metal in question
has exactly the same effect on the producer, whether the
tribute has to be paid in lead or gold, what has been the
most surprising attitude of debtor-Governments towards this
question ?

Not only have they done nothing to encourage an increase
in the supply of gold, but they have, themselves, gone into
the market and, setting up a gold standard and coinage,
raised the price of gold against themselves and their own
subjects, by making that scarcer and dearer which was
already scarce and dear enough.

You will say " this was the work of madmen "; and so it
would have been if it had been done by the people themselves;
it was not, however, done by the people but by the Governments. The Governments were in a difficult position. The
interest on their debts had to be paid in gold. They
received their revenue in silver or paper, and they had
to pay every year more silver and more paper in order
to buy the same amount in gold. What was to be
done? Increase the taxes? No; increase of taxation
breeds discontent. Discontent turns out Governments,
and self - preservation is the first law of nature. If a
man had to pay ten florins or ten francs or ten thalers
where he paid eight before, he could not help knowing that
his taxes were increased ; but if he still continued to pay
eight florins or eight francs or eight thalers on a gold-basis,
he thought he was paying the same amount, although his
real loss, measured by the sacrifice of produce he had to

make, was very likely much greater than the difference between eight and ten.

Probably he had to sacrifice twelve pounds of wool or twelve quarters of wheat or twelve tons of iron or lead or tin where he had only to sacrifice eight before. But the fall in the price of produce was not ascribed to the Government— though the burden of taxation, or in other words the sacrifice of produce by the taxpayer, was really increased by 50 per cent.

What the taxpayers abroad actually did was to call on their Governments for heavy protective duties, which were accordingly imposed and still exist, causing great injury and loss to manufacturers in England. It is difficult to blame the Governments, as they were in a very difficult position, and we must never forget that it has been the action of England, and England alone, which has prevented an international agreement being come to which would have put an end to all these difficulties. Personally, I think foreign Governments are most to blame for not having had the pluck to form an international agreement for the use of silver and gold among themselves together with the United States of America, leaving out England altogether. However that may be, I cannot help thinking that the divergence of value between silver and gold has been almost an unmixed evil to all gold-using countries outside England.

Now let us take the case of England and try to find some compensating advantages for the loss of employment to her manufacturers and workmen. You may naturally say, what other countries lost England must have gained. England is on the balance a creditor-country. If other countries have had to pay more produce to liquidate the annual interest on their gold debt, England must have received more.

But what is England—or the United Kingdom, if you prefer it? A foreign State has to pay interest on a *national* debt which affects the whole body of taxpayers. The State in England has no national investments abroad—receives no interest from abroad. The State has no property, nothing but debts, and very large debts, too ; and in consequence of the scarcity of gold everyone in England who has to pay a portion of the annual interest on the National Debt has to sacrifice a great deal more of his produce than he used to do.

You may say gold is not scarce because there is a great deal in the Bank of England ; and, no doubt, if you want to *borrow* somebody else's gold on good security you can borrow it very easily at a low rate of interest. But try and get some gold for your own by selling a field, or a house, or a few quarters of corn, or some lead, or tin, or iron, or some cotton or linen or jute goods, and you will soon find out whether gold is cheap and plentiful or not.

It is evident it is not the State that gains by the fall in the value of produce. Who is it, then, you mean when you talk of England gaining ? You mean certain individual lenders of money resident in this country. And have they gained ? On the whole, I should doubt it. So many Governments municipalities and individuals in foreign countries have either gone bankrupt, repudiated or reduced the interest on their debts, and so many more seem likely to do so if the fall in silver continues, that I should doubt if the general body of individual lenders of money in this country has really benefited by the divergence in value between gold and silver, and the consequent fall of prices.

We may admit at once that those who are receiving their interest in full are benefiting very largely, and in a way they never expected when they lent the money ; every 100 sovereigns they receive in interest now commanding double as much wheat, wool, tea, silver, iron, lead, tin, and many other things as it did formerly.

Then there is another class who at any rate think they benefit by the present state of things, and that is the class of London bankers and financiers. They say that the fact that London is the only market in the world where gold can always be obtained in large quantities and with ease, is an advantage to them, and has helped to make London the financial centre of the world. It is possible that they are right, and that the present system enriches lenders of, and dealers in, money. On the other hand, this very fact of our stock of gold being open at all times to attack from any quarter is a very great disadvantage to the producing classes of this country who are all borrowers of money, because a sudden demand for gold from any quarter of the world may send up suddenly the rate of discount, though there may be nothing in the state of affairs in England to cause or warrant a rise.

Now I do not myself believe that London could remain the financial centre of the world if she lost her manufactures, and, consequently, a large portion of her trade ; but do we wish to see our producers disappear from this country, even if it were to become the paradise of individual lenders of money and financiers of various nationalities ?

Now I can fancy I hear someone object " but England would always produce *something*. Even if our cottons, and woollens, and linens, and most of our other manufactures are banished, we shall still produce something. They will send us all these things from abroad, and we shall have to send them something in return."

But, my friend, that is exactly where you make a mistake ; and one of the very matters which I think we ought to keep most prominently before us in discussing this matter, is the restriction of our exports, owing to the indebtedness of certain foreign individuals and Governments to individual lenders of money in this country, and the very serious way in which the rise in the value of gold has increased and aggravated this restriction.

In the very short space I have at my disposal I can only indicate the limits within which this restriction works. If no one ever lent any money to any foreign individual or Government, and no long credit were given in international trade, it is evident that the imports and exports (including the precious metals) would exactly balance one another.*

But from the first occasion on which an individual in this country lent £100 to someone abroad, something in the way of cash or produce (and we know practically that all interest from abroad is paid in produce) had to be sent to England in satisfaction of the interest on the debt, and for this nothing in the shape of export goes out in return.

This has gone on until the income, drawn by individual lenders of money from foreign Governments, companies, and individuals, or sent here as a return on capital invested abroad, amounts, it is estimated, to about 100 millions sterling annually, and of course in return for this hundred millions' worth of imports no exports go out.

The limit of this restriction on our exports would, of course, be reached, if individual lenders of money resident in England (or, of course, individuals associated as companies) could get every other nation of the world so deeply into their debt, that all the inhabitants of those countries would have to work as their serfs, sending to England annually, in satisfaction of the interest on their debts, everything they could produce beyond the bare necessaries of life. There could then be no exports from England ; because if all other nations had to send all their surplus produce to England in

* Of course there would always be payments to private individuals, or companies, for personal services, shipping, freights, &c., abroad ; and sums of money would be carried from one country to another by emigrants and immigrants ; but these payments would tend to balance one another, and would not interfere with the general principle.

satisfaction of their debt, they could send nothing in exchange for our exports. This is, of course, the extreme limit that could be reached in theory, and will never be reached in practice. But every fall in the gold-price of commodities carries us nearer and nearer to it.

The price of some of our great staple articles of import, such as wheat, wool, iron, lead and tin have fallen more than one-half during the last twenty years; consequently, double the amount of them has to be sent to satisfy the interest due to individual lenders of money in this country; that is, double the amount of the products of other countries come into this country without any exports going out in exchange for them.

Of course, if gold rises still more in value, and these commodities fall another one-half, then, four times as much of the surplus products of other countries will be at the disposal of individual lenders of money, and the restriction of our exports will be increased fourfold.

The more that silver and other produce fall in value the more commodities produced by cheap labour abroad will be thrown upon our markets in competition with our home-industries, and be sent here merely as interest upon debts, for which nothing whatever is exported in return.

Besides, what we want is as many industries as possible established here on the soil of England. Foreign trade is good, but it is good because it is *trade*, not because it is *foreign*. Home trade is much better. What does foreign trade mean? It means one set of producers living in England, another set of producers living abroad, and these two sets of producers exchanging their products. What does home trade mean? It means two sets of producers, both living in England and exchanging their products. If there were a manufactory of silk established at Calais, and exchanging the finished silk exclusively with England, that would be good. But it would be better if an English capitalist purchased the business, transported the machinery to Dover, and set up an English manufactory, with English workmen there instead.

" Why," you may say, " would it be better, supposing the price of the finished silk remained the same ? The silk would then exchange for exactly the same amount of commodities produced in England as before." That is true of the *products*, but how about the *producers* ?

Every one employed by the factory, in the first case, would be living in France, living in French houses, wearing French clothes, eating French food, using French railways and French banks, paying French taxes, and fighting French battles in time of war.

In the second case, every one employed in the factory would be living in England, in English houses, wearing English clothes, eating English food, using English railways and English banks, paying English taxes, and fighting for England in time of war.

Is there no advantage in having both sets of producers living in England, even in the cases where for what we import we export something in exchange ?

To hear some people talk one is driven to the conclusion that their wish and aim for the future of the United Kingdom is that it should become as quickly as possible a country where no wheat is grown, no barley and no oats ; where no sheep are shorn and no cattle fattened (I suppose they would keep a few cows to supply milk and a few hens to lay fresh eggs for the families of capitalists); where no cotton, no linen, worsteds or woollens would be manufactured ; where all mines and all industries of iron and steel would be closed and idle ;—a country where no one could afford to live except

G

individual lenders of money to other countries and their servants, everything they wanted in the way of commodities being sent them cheaper from abroad than it could be produced in this country, and sent not in return for exports but in satisfaction of the interest on their debts.

If this is the ideal of the English working man he has nothing to do but to sit still and allow our present monetary system to continue, and he will have the satisfaction of feeling that his inaction is helping to bring it to pass, without even the trouble of using his vote.

If his sons and his grandsons in a few years' time abuse him for having allowed employments and manufactories to be banished from England, which, if he had exerted himself to use his vote, might easily have been retained, he will at any rate have the satisfaction of feeling that he has avoided the risk of giving himself a headache by studying dry subjects too deeply.

And now I will say to anyone who has followed me thus far, that I hope my giving this prize has fulfilled one of its objects, that is to say, to induce him to take an interest in the subject; and I hope he will not leave it until he has thoroughly made up his mind how employment in England is likely to be affected by the fact that 100 ounces of silver will now buy as much labour in China as it did prior to 1873.

That during the fifty years before 1873 it took £25 to buy 100 ounces of silver.

That in 1895 it takes little over £11 to buy 100 ounces of silver.

That in consequence of this, labour in a cotton mill in the East now costs less than half as much in English sovereigns as it did for fifty years before 1873, and if the reader is convinced, as I am, that a continued fall in the price of silver means the banishment of the great manufacturing industries of the world from the soil of the United Kingdom to the soil of India, China, Japan and Mexico, to be carried on by Indian, Chinese, Japanese and Mexican workmen instead of the workmen of England, Ireland, Scotland and Wales, then I hope he will recognise his obligation, as a genuine lover of his country, to do all in his power to promote a speedy reform of the present most unsatisfactory monetary conditions of the world.

H. M. MEYSEY-THOMPSON.

THE IRON TRADE AND THE FALL IN THE VALUE OF SILVER.

The Consular report of Mr. Hall, H.B.M.'s Consul at Hako-date, Yezo (one of the Japanese islands), has just been issued as a Parliamentary paper, and the following extract from it may be of interest to English manufacturers, especially those engaged in the iron and steel industries:—
" In conclusion, the broad fact revealed by the statistics is that whilst the industry and home trade of the island is prospering apace, the foreign trade is declining. The cause of such a phenomenon is usually more difficult to ascertain than the fact itself; but in the present instance a concrete case may serve to indicate in what direction the cause is to be looked for. Seven years ago, when this port was supplied with water-works, some 1,500 tons of iron pipes were im-ported from England at a cost of £4 4s., then equal to 28 dollars a ton. This year, owing to the rapid growth of the town, a second parallel line of pipes is required; and if ordered from England the cost would be £4, equal to 40 dollars, a ton, the value of silver as against commodities in this country having in the interval remained virtually the same. No wonder that the native manufacture of iron pipes is being pushed on amain. And this is an example of what is going on all along the line of imports from England and the West. The chasm between the two masses of the world's currency, created by the West's recent expulsion of silver, is acting as a subtle, automatic protective tariff to the silver using countries of the East, checking, on the one side, the growth of trade, and changing, on the other, the natural economic course of industries. The apprehension that gold money would be driven out of use if linked along with silver

as legal tender is alleged as the main reason for the toleration of this block in the channel of the world's business. The question is doubtless a complicated one, on which only experts and competent intellects are entitled to be heard. Sir Isaac Newton, when Master of the Mint, had occasion to consider it; and it is on record that he believed that the apprehended evil could be obviated by the expedient of establishing a par of exchange between the two metals the same for all countries."

www.ingramcontent.com/pod-product-compliance
Lightning Source LLC
Chambersburg PA
CBHW031455270326
41930CB00007B/1016